HOWLING INTO THE VOID

POEMS BY R. DAVID FULCHER

OLD SCRATCH PRESS

HOWLING INTO THE VOID

Cover and design: David Yurkovich

ISBNs:

978-1-957224-72-5 (paper)
978-1-957224-73-2 (digital)

Library of Congress Control Number: 2026934972

This is a work of poetry. Names, characters, and incidents are either products of the author's imagination or used fictitiously.

Published by Old Scratch Press, an imprint of Current Words Publishing, LLC, Los Angeles, CA.

Find us at:
oldscratchpress.com
currentwords.com

This chapbook is dedicated to my beautiful wife Lisa,

my muse in all things.

ALSO BY R. DAVID FULCHER

FICTION

Asteroid 6 and Other Tales of Cosmic Horror

The Pumpkin King and Other Tales of Terror

Trains to Nowhere and Other Stories of World War II

Blood Spiders and Dark Moon: Tales of Horror, Science Fiction and Fantasy

The Cemetery of Hearts: More Stories of Horror, Fantasy and Science Fiction

The Lighthouse at Montauk Point and Other Stories

NONFICTION

The Movies That Make You Scream!

CONTENTS

HOWLING INTO THE VOID

PERCEPTION

You who do not
believe
that angels dance
on pinheads
tell me that
rainbows
are not contained
in prisms
that love does not
lie
in the shadows
of photographs
that you do not
lie.

Nothing
exists in a single state.
I am not
contained by these walls.

I can shrink and reside

in the dirty hovel
of a bottle
I can expand and reside
in the mansion of verse.

R. David Fulcher

OVErgroWth

Once there was a forest spring
Where Pan did dance and his pipes did sing
The woodland creatures, boar and deer
Would bow their heads and revere
The water clear and Pan's ear.

When each had had their delicious fill
Dance like drunkards, tumble and spill
Anthropomorphic one would think
Strange behavior from special drink
Pan has told me he's seen them wink.

Years have grown and closed that road
To where Pan and his pipes became betrothed
Man was meant to lose the path
For he forsook what nature hath
Turned forest spring into boiling bath.

mElinda

Sometimes in the lonely hours
I would walk the hill
Leaving the clamor and din behind
For headstones grey and still.

As I neared the place where the dead do lie
I knelt and bowed my head
A fool is he who visits the graves
Without homage to the dead.

'Melinda' read the stone I sought
Melinda, my betrothed,
Only a thief as clever as Death
Could steal the health of Melinda, my love.

Often I hear Melinda's voice
Soft upon the breeze
I answer her call of eternal love
And grow hoarse among the trees.

R. David Fulcher

 sky city

(based on the history of the Zuni Indian pueblo of Acoma in New Mexico)

Acoma, the Zuni Masada
Defiantly cuts and opens the sky
Revealing dark blue innards.

Coronado came.
Young men fed the thirsty mesa
With heavy blood which held the dust.

Coronado conquered.
Odious timbers were dragged to the mesa top
Then erected to build a shrine
A shrine for the holy and the devilish as well.

Proud Coronado!
You came and you conquered.
But did your soul ever yearn to ascend the ladders to the
great, dark, blue heavens?
That great blue sheet which covered and smothered you.

Eating

Robert Penn Warren
writes, "we must
eat our dead."
Perhaps, but the food
of the living
is already
on the table—
Can't we freeze
the dead
and eat them
tomorrow night?

Can't we put off
breathing
false aromas of denial
for a time
of personal famine?
Can't we avoid
the tough steaks of grief
until we are ready
to soften them
with thyme and honey?

Must we eat them
at all?
Can't we turn up our noses
at those pale faces
which clash so starkly

with the checkered
tablecloth
turn to one another
and say: "Who
could eat
at a time
like this?"

skylight: NEW mEXiCO

The spheres I thought jewels were only of brass
I should have known, reeling through desert sky
Beauty is only as deep as the mask.

Rattler or rodent I meant no trespass
Here only to feel the truth of the lie
The spheres I thought jewels were only of brass.

Guised in piety like monks of days past
God himself knew, portraying painted eyes
Beauty is only as deep as the mask.

The choral coyotes mocked with their laugh
I sought the voice to howl back in reply
The spheres I thought jewels were only of brass!

The still cactus oblivious to wrath
I thought the spiny thing strong to defy
God and his guises, coyotes, and masks.

I bled like a virgin in the desert scrub grass
Never again a midnight passerby.
The spheres I thought jewels were only of brass
The beauty revealed was only a mask.

R. David Fulcher

Air-Crash

Epigraph: "METAL MYTH LIES BROKEN IN WOODS"
Phoenix 747.
Oh Great Bird, your fires were as bold
as the flames of Prometheus—
Was it he that snapped your wings in
a fit of jealousy?
His laughter which shrieked
and receded in the black box
as you tumbled earthward?

midnight visitor

Around midnight I hear a scratching at my windows.
Who would come to my depressing warehouse of memories
so full of ghost aisles and boxed skeletons?
Only one person comes to mind
but when the snow was still fresh upon the ground
we transferred hatreds and slammed doors to make our words
official.

Rising out of bed I move along the wall shadow-like
and in one quick motion snap back the curtain:
It's only a cat, mistaking my life for a darkened alley.

R. David Fulcher

song of self

Listen lost children to the Sirens of memory
Their call parts the fog which shrouds the sunflower
and the speech of seasons

The will-o-wisp will guide you into the fringe
Through grey forests to the glade of beginnings
Where your seed is entwined with the seed of the sunflower
Where the monsters of myth tear at your consciousness

You will try to remember what lies beyond the shapeless forest
You will try to remember and you will forget

Hear the covens of Salem dance naked and wild
Hear the dark women chant, "The answer is blood, metal and fire."
Hear the prayer wheels spin softly from the roof of the world
Hear the high winds murmur, "The answer is ice and the humble
discovery."
Hear negroes beat verse of tribal ancestry
Hear the drums vibrate, "The jungle is good for it is wild and terrible."

Follow the soft light as the will-o-wisp beckons you
Through the labyrinths of dream and personal myth
Hear the Sirens howl through the chaos of imagery
Hear the sweet voice of the infant deity

GrEEn PastUrEs

I'm not fool enough to believe
that there never comes a time
when one must leave the green pastures
and the music behind
to fight for their beliefs
in a man-made hell
It's just that I rebel against it
that's all
I worry about those who
go in with a fanatical eagerness
with a "I'm gonna kill me a commie" look
on their faces
They've never seen what I've seen
or it least it didn't mean the same thing to them
if they saw it
I would like nothing more
than to never leave the green pastures
just leave my soul up there in the cirrus
and think nothing but feel everything
The battles I would contemplate
would be no bigger than Thoreau's ants
At least it would be a natural conflict
devoid of the insanity of man
Sometimes I feel like a scarlet crab
hanging on the rocks beside the sea
which threatens to sweep me away
before I release my brown multitudes
of conception

R. David Fulcher

Sometimes I yearn to drown in those waves
and know of the peace
beyond the green pastures

HOOPS

It wasn't the easy, fluid style of play you see on TV

It was the jerky, nervous style of amateurs

played on asphalt several feet away from where I was sitting.

My shorts had ripped horrendously down the back during the last game

but that really didn't matter in the big scheme of things

and besides, the jocky guy Chris would have never

picked me to play after screwing up the last game so badly.

An observer watched the game from the other side of the court

grinning to himself secretly.

Perhaps he was happy to see the different bodies working so well together, Van, the Vietnamese; Joy, the Indian; Greg the black guy and Danny the Anglo; or perhaps that was just what I wanted to see.

It didn't really matter in the big scheme of things. Nothing really does.

Chris the jock made a three-pointer, and murmurs of approval such as, "Good shot, man" or "Nice one, Chris" fill the air

replacing the sound of the tennis shoes against the pavement.

I never questioned Chris' basketball prowess.

It was his attitude that puzzled me.

I wanted to shake him and say, "Hey, Chris! Listen to what I'm saying, man! You're just a pebble in the stream, man! Just a lowly grain of salt! This shot won't change the world, dig?"

But you can't tell a guy like Chris something that big.

He would just laugh it off and call you a stinkin' liberal hippie,

and go about his business of shooting politically correct jump shots while I would go about my business of trying to change the things that couldn't be changed, things that really didn't matter anyway.

R. David Fulcher

EntEr thE TEnth mUSE

She walks softly where the zephyrs beckon
         her
Through tufts of flowers which blush pink at
         her passage.
The springs capture her
Her visage displayed like a gem set in
         silver.
Lilacs fall upon her brow—snow which never
         melts
In her supple palm that holds the world in
         its grasp.

Afternoon Walker

Your hands are brittle, like ice mittens.
your steps cautious, as if you stand on
the lip of the world, swaying, kite-like
over that bright abyss Youth, willing
yet not willing to fall and forget
those sunlit visions of dance and love
that bitter salt hatred, that calloused
tyrant Age. Is that what guides you through
this maze of Chevys, Fords and Volvos
day after day, another machine
who has forgotten its instructions
but runs on, until the motor stops?

R. David Fulcher

ThE TrEES BEhind the Old HOUSE

They are going to tear down the trees behind the old house
Which will surely drive away the ghosts or at least the squirrels
>who enjoyed the sanctuary of those stoic lords.
I shall miss their raspy, plaintive speech
They told me much because they told me little
And only when the wind beckoned them to speak.
Oh God, how different it was from the incessant chattering of folks
>Every creak of their limbs philosophy
>Every rustle of their garments poetry.

still, I turn my Ear to sunflowers

It was a time when
everything seemed big
Especially the lords of my
father's garden, the sunflowers.
They towered over me and the
tomato plants, enjoying equal
authority over both.
For hours I would stand listening
Cupped ear toward the comfortable
brown seeds which were as cozy
as roosting bats.
Every day of summer I listened
Certain that their patient speech
would reveal the secrets of their wisdom.

My life has taken me far from that garden
Those wizened, brown faces
That time when everything seemed big.
Somewhere along the road I learned that sunflowers
      never talked
And that adults should neither desire nor expect
      such a thing to pass.
Yet perhaps the fact that I still turn
      cupped ear to sunflowers
Perhaps this says something also.

R. David Fulcher

CrEatiON POEM

in the beginning
they promised light
muted, invasive
it filtered to our depths

we flowed towards it
like a collective thought
or a lazy dream
in a mad god's eye

now energy-suffused
we broke the waves
here, there
scattering like lost children

following instinct
before instinct
existed

the most ambitious of us
streaked upward
shimmering cousins
pinning up

the cloak of
primordial
night
others

built continents
islands
masses of stone

others lay dying
on newly-formed
beaches

today
you and I
carry those sparks

centuries refined
passion diluted

R. David Fulcher

ThrEE-hUndrEd and sixty

The arrow's strong flight

driven by bloodlust and sweat, is also an insight into that which
spills the tides,

that which strikes, stings, delights, or scares, that which swims, or
flies, or crawls

that which falls to ruin and that which rises to triumph.

If only it could fly full circle!

We would know, we would see, we would shake and tremble

beneath its woody vibrations

as we do before truth.

ThrEE-hUndrEd and sixty

ThE FEar and thE BEauty, NEW mEXiCO

I was utterly terrified of it, the Black Widow which resided
by the doorstep of my brother's apartment.
My brother laughed at my uneasiness
as if I were a schoolboy on his first date.
I remember him going on and on, explaining how
the spider was the embodiment of a benevolent female spirit
or some other such nonsense as we spiraled
down the mountains of Carlsbad, the image
of the bats departing the caverns
still hotly pressed upon our consciousness.
I will never forget the bats, thousands of them
each part of the wild spectacle:
a black river which shot out of the entrance
tornadoed upwards through the dusk
and spilled over the canyon
like a burst of sunlight.

R. David Fulcher

sanctuary

The sun
is falling
in the east
beneath the radio tower
which pulses
in the night
like a red
heartbeat.

Smells of Sunday
dinner waft
down the stairs
on Elven feet
remnants of animal
things
the harvest and
the gentle
sleep.

Kissing the Sky

Shingles coarse on bare foot soles:

I step up to survey the realm of squirrels.

Here there are only branches and breeze

      The sky is something else

      A rooftop of a different sort.

Weary, I lay my back against the warm brickwork

of the chimney which holds up our ghost on Halloween.

There, beyond the apex, lies the runway of my childhood.

There my brother and I would jump with arms

      outstretched like wings

and crash land on shaky legs and grass stains.

R. David Fulcher

If I walk unloved

If I walk unloved it is because my nymph eludes me.
She skips over Andromeda with a pink blushing cheek
while the stars fall like petals at her bare feet.

She dances nimbly on treetops with winged handmaidens
who with garlands of berries are heavily laden.

She steps lightly on rooftops while peasants make mirth
scarcely louder than the fire which breathes in the hearth.

A part of my soul is reserved for her shrine
filled with incense and flowers and Olympian wine
The muses have decorated her temple with verse
but pursuit is her fancy, as well as my curse.

ThE SEa

The windswept sands disperse my thoughts
Of what once was gained but now is lost
The sky, the sand, the sea, the sun
My soul cries out, my will undone
What we had I cannot restore
My dreams sink slowly, the ocean floor.

Her form moves before me, within the waves
A beautiful, dim, and false display
Towards me she moves, and then away
To leave me here in my dismay.
Too confused to think, and too weak to stay
I leave the place where we once lay.

I think no more, it is behind
A distant place, a distant time
A part of me it will always be
The sky, the sand, and the sea.

R. David Fulcher

Living Room magic

Drawing the drapes across the windows completes my
        invocation.
Oh Great One
I remember you from the caves in New Mexico
Stooping low in leathers
Depicting the Great Hunt with limestone vision.

Even then I knew your magic.
Now with beads and hides and makeshift paints I await you.
Show me the wind
And I shall make the walls fall away
I will capture its spirit
And skirl and stomp, hoot and shout
And if my TV is lost in the ritual so be it.

Come quickly
The buffalo thunder across the plains
Like a thousand hailstones.
We will make a fire out of the coffee table and wait.
We will stand on the VCR and draw our bowstrings.
Nothing will be wasted.
Nothing forsaken.

ThE SUiCiDE HOUSE

I remember the coldness
the mortuary chill to the bone
which permeated the walls
floors, and furniture
of that house.
"Goddamn it!" I would say
upon entering the house
"It's freezing in here!"
Then my dad would turn on the heat
Consoling me with the talk of soon-to-come warmth.

But I still felt it.
I could not shake it.

Once it was not cold.
I was warm before I got there
the piles of junk and
the heavy drizzle
hiding the taboo activity
in the back of the Pontiac.
With her there, there was warmth
The unforgiving bed of granite
almost melted.
But still, the chill—
the shiver to remind me
the fire was isolated,
hot coals left behind
to die and extinguish

R. David Fulcher

in a living room fireplace.
I cannot forget.
I will never forget
those nights I spent tense
alert, laid out like stone on the bed
waiting for that goddamn chill to envelop me
the chill of the woman who took her life
the woman who was found sprawled out
on the tile floor
which received her last kiss.
I cannot forget.
I will never forget
the chill.

Confessions of a Wood Guitar

Men have loved me since I was a crude, one-stringed thing
For it is to me that they come in the dead of night
When their souls are like vases without flowers.

I alone await their caresses
Their gentle rhythms which drive me to music.
Some arouse my passion to great themes and movement
Others use me basely; choking my wooden neck while I shriek
     and wail.
The quiet ones are content to hold my frame against
     their own.

I, none other, console the truly lonely heart
and for this I am locked away in a dusky black coffin
exhumed for the pleasure of men, and buried again.

R. David Fulcher

stars

The stars fell on me tonight
Whether it took an age or an hour
I cannot be sure.

But they fell.

They fell and grew huge in my vision
Cobalt will-o-wisps beckoning me
To an existence of cool distance.

Nights like these
Make me hate my daily ascension
Into sunlight
Nights like these
Let me know
When I die
I will be with the stars.

ACROSTIC BLUES

(for Robert Johnson)

Rusty bluesman
On a porch in Mississippi
Back door embraces
Envy of the levy.
Run, boy, run.
The crossroads are waiting.

Jugular bulging:
Oh, I'm a steady rollin' man
Half-step bends on
Neck of Maplewood
Son of the Delta
Over whose hot words died your
Never-ending song

R. David Fulcher

Aging, Act I

I am old and forgotten
like a picture
that was never framed
or a country fence
in disrepair

I call my youth
back to me
but he resists
languishing drunk
on Spring and sunlight
chasing ageless nymphs
across fields of heather

I weep my bones
out on the table
but no one comes
to check out the rattle and bang
or sweep up the dust which falls
from my eyes

Aging, Act II

Youth is an ugly thing
like the limp feathers of a gull
lost to the sea's turgent burst of breath.
Perhaps, when the storm has past
and Apollo appraises me with his circumspect eye
perhaps then I will know beauty's hidden places
those elder glades where Triumph hides her face
like a coy mistress and where birds of paradise
loose their plumage like a thousand suns.

R. David Fulcher

WhilE I SlEEp

Here, while I sleep, I will speak with runic insight
Icons and archetypes will slide off my tongue smooth as song
While reels turn over plastic achievements—
      click and whir, click and whir—
         awake.

Dorothy's Dead

Ears muffled, head down, I walk like a decayed thing
Metallic perhaps, a tin man without a heart
Alien to the earthy crispness.
Nothing moves on the dead field
The blanket of frost like the shroud of a corpse
The numbing cold like the pain of loss.

I approach the tattered scarecrow
His ragged, worn face is set like weathered stone
Forever set gazing into a sea of grey sky.
Weary friend, what do those hollow sockets see?
A lonely man flailing in the pungent froth of a raging corn field?

Yes, I know my friend, metal does not float.

R. David Fulcher

Rain Day

The trees scrape
the sky's underbelly with raw limbs
as the prow of a school bus
rises above the swamped street
the faces of sparrow-like children
pressed against the panes
as if going to execution.

Today, even the leaves have lost their will to fly.

Stoic houses hold their breaths
their shades drawn tight as eyelids
and shiver with woody creaks and groans
as they wait for Spring.

I take it in long draughts
all this yearning to be carried away
not to the haven of sparrows
but to the moist grave of Autumn.

 HUNTER

I smell the beast below me
and I descend through the dense canopy
like rustling leaves
my membranes extended for silent glide.
How terrible I must be
to that panting thing below
Black, absolute, like a falling piece of night.

It runs, panicked, and stumbles in the undergrowth
Fleeing from my shrieks of delight
My glistening fangs like needle-thin twins
It too knows what must come to pass.

The rapture is indescribable
Pure intoxication on salty red wine
Which courses freely beneath the
pealy cork of skin.
Satisfied at last, I ascend
into the cover of night
Gliding peacefully above the treetops
until I hunt again.

R. David Fulcher

ThE Bat

Taking inverted Sabbath in the Caverns of Carlsbad
I measure time in locust-breath and calcite drip
My bird-chest rising and falling with the gentle tides
Of this black carpet of brotherhood.

Footsteps fill my dreams
Sun-bleached tourists groping into the cavern's belly
To enter the sublime
Their voices like a million valves releasing pressure.
For an instant they will recognize the face of God in this hard
       darkness
The stalactite points of his beard
The cascading stone formations of his brow
And that fraction of animal intellect will rush forth
Freed from concept and equation
To join our ranks as we veer through this Jerusalem darkness.
Towards dusk and sustenance
Towards the amphitheater where the people wait for their own
departure.

THE SLOW PEOPLE OF THE SWAMP

The boats hang nestled against the dock
motionless, like still-born children
waiting for morning and motion.
I am still, ears pressed against the weedy mouth of the swamp
following the speech of cypress
and the slap of gator tail.
A light illumines a shape sliding down the bayou
and by the measured creak of the oarlocks
I recognize it as human
one of those who lives within the swamp
one of the slow dumb folk they call swamp rats.
His muscles and breath
move as his people have always moved through this swamp
effortlessly, one with the secretive eyes of the raccoon
and the slither of water moccasins.
Tomorrow, or perhaps the next day
they shall drain this stretch of swamp
big men with ugly machines
who will uproot the trees and tear away the green veil of vines.

But that is tomorrow.
Tonight I shall listen to the swamp and its kin
and wish to know what the slow dumb folk know.

R. David Fulcher

Gawkers

The whole beach watches like a single eye
gasping and pointing
wrapped in bikinis and Speedos
lotions and sunglasses.
There's a body on the waves
floating on its back like a sleeper.
Its limbs move listless and bloated
in time with the ebb and flow of the water.

The gulls wheel and screech through the sky
Wild, animate kites without attachments.
These other came later—
bearing swords of cotton candy
and Coppertone
erecting striped wildflowers
which close before nightfall.
They have come
to claim the beach.

Even the sea rejects them.

A spidEr's Thanksgiving

You stride boldly across the wall
Your limbs rising and falling like miniature strikes of
lightning Searching for a corner you call home.

You lower yourself on silky threads
Your pulleys well-oiled and silent
Your forelegs propelling you downwards
In a vertical breaststroke.
You dance across gossamer girders
Tending to your geometric dining hall.

I stand there poised with a broomstick
When a fly strikes your resilient web.
Kick and turn, kick and turn—the fly is furious.
But you are casual
Sauntering across your fragile network
Your head a death-grin
Your mandibles wet with anticipation.

R. David Fulcher

October Sestina

Colors crunched, Autumn hues on painted leaves
I shifted to take you in under the late sunlight.
Clouds of breath sailed away, their warmth berating the air.
The lake was a mirror, recognizing dusk and its stillness
Our pile of oranges and yellows was recently scattered by children
The same children who play at every leaf pile in our minds as ghosts.

The darkness came gradually, building a haunting for ghosts
who lived on the fringes of darkness, fearful of the fingers of
sunlight.
A nocturnal breeze came out of hiding to disturb the stillness
and to wrestle with the branches to forfeit their leaves.
The leaves plastered our hair, and we laughed like children
Not sensing our vulnerability to the cutting air.

I can smell those woods in the air
And I can see it in the way the leaves
Spiral down, down, down through the late sunlight
like stones onto the mirror lake, shattering its stillness.
I can see the fragments spinning crazily upwards towards the
children
And their screams echoing through the woods and disappearing like
ghosts.

The wind through the trees sounds like stirring ghosts
or perhaps more like the hushed screams of captured sunlight
and when I walk through the woods at night I step on the leaves
cautiously, careful not to break the lake's children
with a thousand spinning fragments of stillness

which cut invisibly like ghosts through the air.

All Hallow's Eve, and the mystery in the air
comes with images of goblins, witches, and ghosts.
This holiday has never been one for sunlight.
And it's easy to forget that the pirates and demons are mere children
carrying their orange and yellow bags like so many leaves.
I've never seen that night achieve its desired stillness.

Before Dawn raises her pink, flushed face displacing the stillness
with the extension of long, slender fingers of sunlight
turning the vampires into dust and distilling the ghosts
into dirty sheets and sleepy-eyed children.
Just like last year, and the year before, the leaves
spiral down, down, down through the air.

R. David Fulcher

 LOVE

Love is delivered
in a steel-blue carriage
by a peach-colored nymph
who rests on silks
and sucks on stems of cherries
flinging the pits out the window
to her victims who writhe
and choke in the dust.

OdE to thE NiGht

To the Night, the Night, the dark delight
The children sleep soundly in gentle white
Breathing in time with the Raven's flight.

To the Night, the Night, the waxen moon
Audience of one to the witches' croon
Driving the tides for the sailors' doom.

To the Night, the Night, its starlit fires
Which guide the ghosts from funeral pyres
Which soften the Harpy to play the lyre.

R. David Fulcher

 war--

The trees were bent
and their shadows slain
in last night's battle
between wind and rain.

Winter Sestina

The fields are full of dead flowers
Heads bowed and heavy like shackled ghosts
Shambling towards the roadside.
Cars choke out the white noise of the sun
Their grilles belching dirty thunder
Which burns the hand of silence.

Children sleep in flannel silence
Their eyelids closed flowers
Which flicker beneath sensory thunder.
Snowflakes fall unnoticed, crystalline ghosts
Which haunt the reaches of the sun
Then die by the roadside.

A thousand eyes watch the roadside
Yawns ripple the silence
As the metal tide flows towards the sun.
The cold forges the bitterness of flowers
Never bought or lovers who embrace as living ghosts.
The low choppy skies herald no thunder.

Children scramble up slopes, their feet muffled thunder
As they speed on waxed runners toward the roadside.
The sick ones stay inside, their ecstasy only a ghost
As they watch the cold celebration in windowed silence.

Lovers sleep like joined flowers
Temporarily oblivious to the death of the sun.

R. David Fulcher

Alley cats curl in newspapers, their eyes miniature suns
Which flare in time to the urban thunder.
Children make snow angels, the flowers
Of their cheeks red like the soda cans which litter the roadside.
Bums sleep on grates in silence
Haunted by bottles, invisible as ghosts.

Cars sleep in snowdrifts like dinosaur ghosts
Waiting to be freed by the sun.
A film of ice covers all as the silence
Lowers and blankets cover the thunder
Of hearts. Empty, the roadside
Sighs and dreams of flowers.

The ghost of the sun waits behind the thunder
Shedding petals of fire
Which collect silently by the roadside.

Chivalry

I would discard my chainmail and arms if I thought they would not
be needed
Lay them gently down in some far pasture
As if I were putting an animal to final rest.
Then I would walk lightly away
And let the soft murmurings of time woo their memory from my soul
Putting them to final rest like a brook burying pebbles.

Acknowledgement

I wish to acknowledge David Yurkovich and Dianne Pearce for their continued support and confidence in my work. Without them, this book would not have been possible.

My heartfelt appreciation also goes out to Virginia Watts and Beatriz Fernandez for editing this manuscript.

About the Author

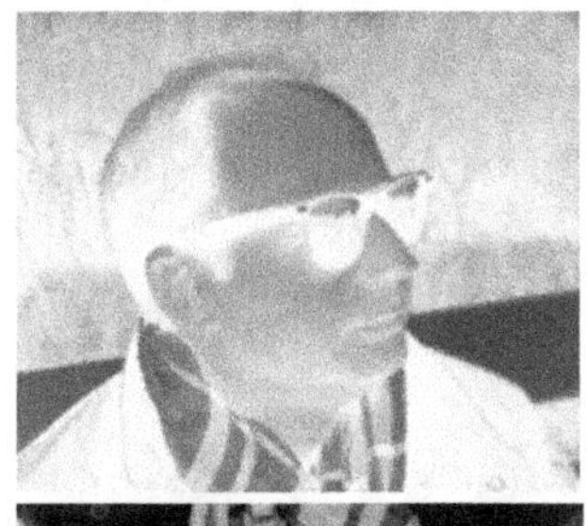
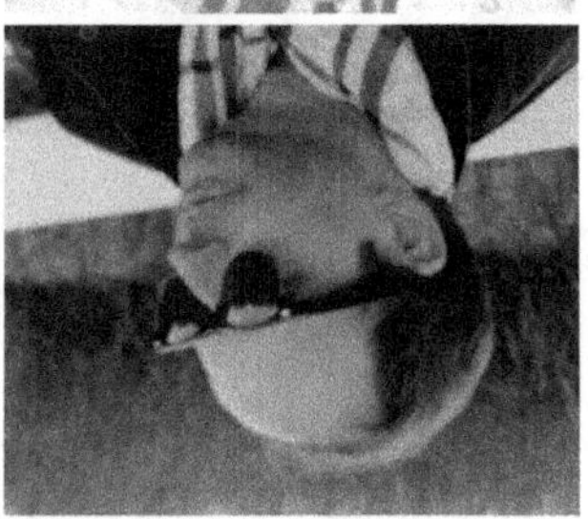

R. David Fulcher is an author of horror, science fiction, fantasy, and poetry. Major literary influences include H.P. Lovecraft, Dean Koontz, Edgar Allen Poe, Fritz Lieber, and Stephen King.

He is the author of several collections, including *The Lighthouse at Montauk Point and Other Stories, The Pumpkin King and Other Tales of Terror*, and the award-winning *Asteroid 6 and Other Tales of Cosmic Horror*.

His work can also be found in the anthologies *Hard-Boiled and Loaded with Sin* (Hawkshaw), *Halloween Party 2019* (Devil's Party), and *Halloween Party '21* (Gravelight).

More at rdavidfulcher.com

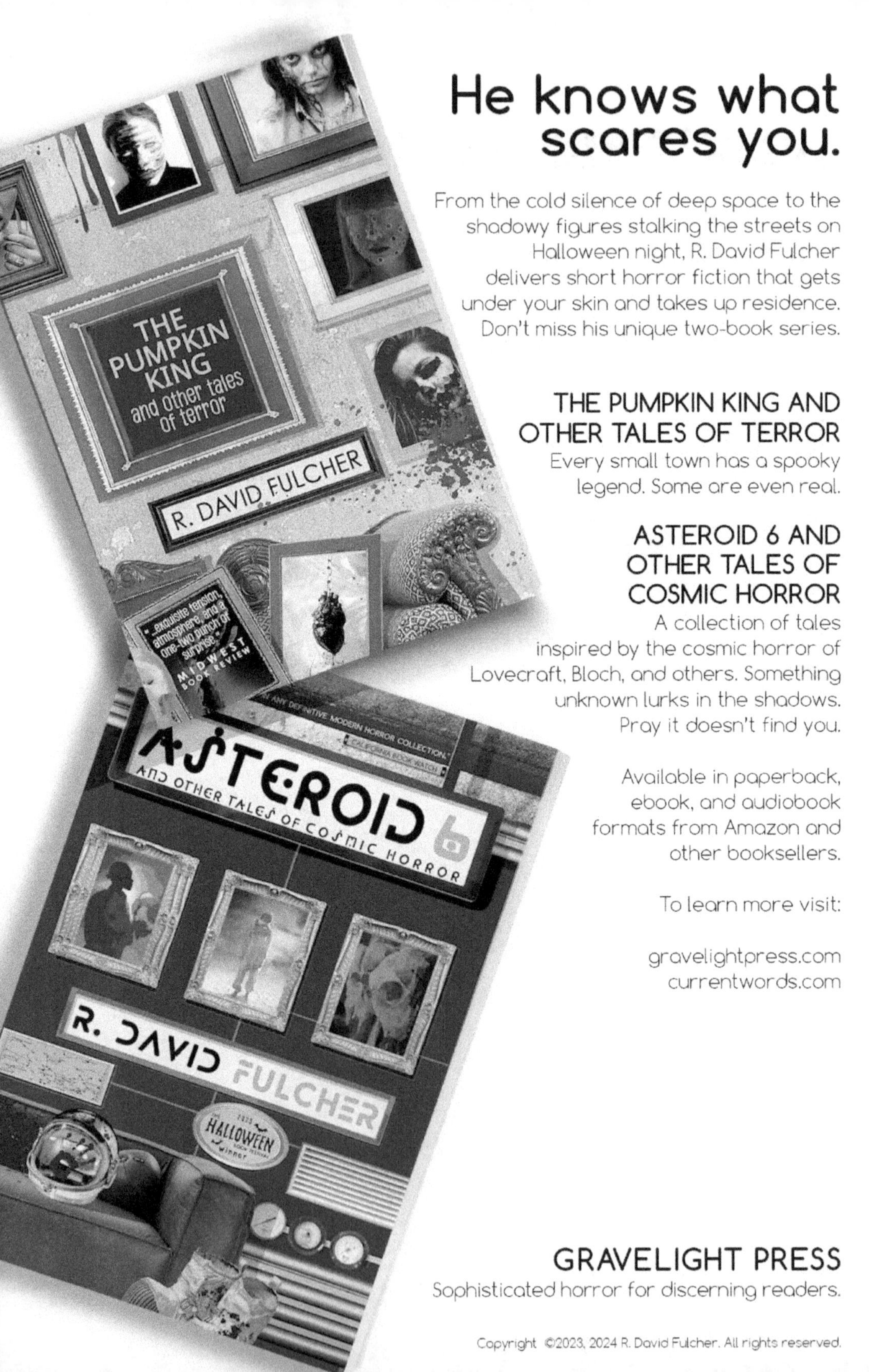

He knows what scares you.

From the cold silence of deep space to the shadowy figures stalking the streets on Halloween night, R. David Fulcher delivers short horror fiction that gets under your skin and takes up residence. Don't miss his unique two-book series.

THE PUMPKIN KING AND OTHER TALES OF TERROR

Every small town has a spooky legend. Some are even real.

ASTEROID 6 AND OTHER TALES OF COSMIC HORROR

A collection of tales inspired by the cosmic horror of Lovecraft, Bloch, and others. Something unknown lurks in the shadows. Pray it doesn't find you.

Available in paperback, ebook, and audiobook formats from Amazon and other booksellers.

To learn more visit:

gravelightpress.com
currentwords.com

GRAVELIGHT PRESS

Sophisticated horror for discerning readers.

Poetry for the present moment

Established in 2023, Old Scratch Press is a poetry collective built
on collaboration, mentorship, and shared opportunity.
Our writers come together to create, publish, and support work
that reflects the voices and experiences of today.

Discover new voices, or find your place among them.

Learn more at oldscratchpress.com

OSP
OLDSCRATCHPRESS.COM